Praise for
Make Money with Facebook Groups

"When I wanted to learn how to get the most out of my Facebook group, I turned to Abbie Unger and her new book. This book could be a textbook, but it's not boring like one! It gave me everything I needed to create a thriving group and make some money. Once I started reading, I couldn't put it down. I highly recommend this book."

Kimanzi Constable
Best-selling author of
Are You Living or Existing?

"This book gives great insight into the world of Facebook. Abbie has done a wonderful job in explaining the benefits of groups and makes it easy for the reader to implement her strategies and advice. I would absolutely recommend this book to anyone who needs some inspiration, is willing to put the actions and work into creating successful relationships and wants to use Facebook to leverage their work."

Isabel Hundt
Professional Coach, Speaker, and Author

"I love, love, love this book and have been encouraging members of my team to read it. I keep having "aha" moments and brainstorms. I am excited to try out this concept of building groups to build a tribe and an income! This book has inspired me in so many ways in the past couple of days!"

Rebekah Bain
The Rock Fitness
BeachBody Coach

"This is one of the BEST biz books I have ever read. For a long time, I struggled with really wondering if I am qualified to teach people in a group setting my expertise. Abbie's advice has been invaluable to me. The night I started my Facebook group, I got about 20 requests to join within an hour. A couple of days later, here we are at 50 members and the discussion is strong, supportive and exciting! Don't ever doubt your own genius. Follow the author's advice and go rock your biz with a Facebook group!"

Charity Nicole
The Instagram Rockstar
#InstaHappyRich

"Abbie Unger has written a very clear, concise, and applicable book about how to develop successful Facebook groups. One of my favorite parts was in the beginning when she talked about how her group was not successful and she got frustrated with just having 12 members, I could relate to that! Each chapter is a great step on how to not only build but continued to maximize the effectiveness of your group. I highly recommend this book."

Jennifer Tubbiolo
Best-selling author of
The Narthex Academy Series

"I have had a Facebook Group for quite a while but NEVER thought about monetizing it! Reading Abbie's book helped clarify that I do have something of value to offer the members of my group, so why not capitalize and make it even easier for the members to find that value while making my life easier! I have so many highlighted portions of the book on my Kindle but what really stuck out was this: "When did 'fame' become a four-letter word? When did we start thinking of fame as a negative byproduct of success?" <--- It's so true that we often say fame is a bad thing, yet at its core, we can achieve fame simply by offering answers to people's questions! I would highly recommend this book for anyone who is using social media to further their business ventures!"

Naomi Hattaway
www.NaomiHattaway.com

"This book is a must for ANYONE trying to build their platform or business. I heard Abbie speak at a conference in June and it completely changed my mindset when it comes to the use of Facebook groups. This book gives you amazing tips on growing your audience which will in turn, increase your sales. I have been implementing all of her suggestions and am amazed at the results I'm seeing in such a short time. Very good investment!"

Corie Clark
Creator of
The Purposeful Planner

"Almost everyone is on Facebook, but few seem to have figured out how to monetize it. Abbie Unger takes you through the steps to post on Facebook not just as a casual fan, but as an entrepreneur. Big surprise, it's all about building relationships! The author provides concrete advice with enough encouragement that you'll want to go out right away and start a Facebook group!"

FoodDiva
Online Review

"Honestly, no one could have convinced me that you could make money from a Facebook group. Enter Abbie: She has completely changed my mind. I loved that she broke down what it means to have a healthy group, just like you would a plant. I see that a lot in groups that have no engagement, and eventually, they die off. I checked out Abbie's group: 10,000 members?! That is one healthy group! More than just teaching her readers, Abbie encourages them and knocks down negativity: "When did 'fame' become a four-letter word? When did we start thinking of fame as a negative byproduct of success?" I really encourage anyone with a dream, anyone with a goal, anyone who wants to create something successful—and make money to—to read Abbie's book."

Shayla Eaton
Curiouser Editing

"This is a well thought out discussion of a little known social media tool. Many kinds of entrepreneurs will find ideas here that will directly impact and improve their customer reach and engagement. I personally have been surprised by how well these techniques work."

Dr. John Oakes
Bestselling novelist
The Right Kind of Stupid
Death Pope

"This is a really interesting and encouraging book. I had never considered the idea of using a Facebook group to build a business, but it makes so much sense after reading how the author used a group to build her business. The book also focuses more broadly on encouraging people to pursue their dreams - even if I never create a Facebook group, this book has encouraged me to think about my blog and writing in a new way."

Gaye Christmus
www.calmhealthysexy.com

"Very helpful via tactical tips for Facebook groups. I've grown my group from 50ish people to over 400."

Alex Barker
Author of
Hangout and Grow Rich

"This is an incredible resource! Abbie covers all the ins and outs and walk you through the process of setting up, maintaining and generating income via Facebook groups. Plus how to provide value for those that join, as ultimately that is why someone joins a FB group. Great guide!"

Camilla Kragius
Author and Blogger
No More Hamsters Wheel

"Before I read Abbie's book I wasn't sure I wanted or needed a Facebook group. In her book she does an excellent job explaining the ins and outs of groups. She was able to share her stories of the group she has created to help so many. I read her book in one day and was provided so much valuable information I created a group within a week."

Pamela Gann
Admin of
Moms Offering Other Moms Support

Make Money
with
Facebook Groups

Build Relationships

Convert Customers

Create Fame

Abbie Unger

Cover Design: Kelsey Humphreys

DEDICATION

For the members of Flight Attendant Career Connection.
Especially those who cheered, contributed, and believed from the
beginning.
Christi, Christopher, Janice, Angela, Veronica, Nannette and Nicole.

"Paris, First Class, International"

CONTENTS

To my parents, Chuck and Karey Sumner:
I have the best. You taught me right from wrong, the power of generosity and the beauty of family. I get the entrepreneurial gene honest. A special that you to my copy editor: Mama.

To my brother, Chad Sumner:
My first business partner. When we were children, Chad and I would swim in the pond on the golf course near our house and dig golf balls out of the mud with our toes. After a night of bleach soaking, we would resell the golf balls to golfers on the course. Our success was cut short when an alligator moved into our pond, but the entrepreneurial spirit is still going strong.

To my husband, Jason Unger:
We had only been married a few weeks when you shot down my first crazy business idea but over the years I have seen the power in your stable, risk-adverse outlook. Thank you for always letting me have the spotlight.

To Ty:
You transformed me from a regular girl into the magical creature we call a mother. You are all sweetness and all boy, just like your Daddy. Don't let life harden your tender heart.

To Emily Grace:
Your funny personality and spunk is so much like your Mama. Don't let anyone quiet you down or douse your fire.

To Jet:
I cannot wait to discover who you are. I cannot wait to see who you become.

To Kimanzi Constable:
I would have never reached this level of success without your guidance. Thank you for seeing the big picture, talking me off the ledge, and showing me opportunities that I didn't even think were possible. The best business decision I ever made was to work with you, Coach.

To Kelsey Humphreys:
I am awed at the way you inspire greatness. I love watching your pursuit.

To Brittany from Facebook:
Thank you for discovering me and seeing the true vision of Flight Attendant Career Connection. Thank you for getting it.

INTRODUCTION

*"May your life someday be as awesome
as you pretend it is on
Facebook"*

I Love Facebook Groups

I am not a professionally trained marketing expert. I do not have a degree in computer science, graphic arts, or marketing. In fact, I studied Theology. I'm just a girl with a Facebook account who loves people and is passionate about getting her message in front of as many people as possible so it can help as many people as possible. I tell you this because I want you to know you can do what I did. You don't have to have a degree or special credentials to market your book, company, or message. All you need is a spirit of generosity, the confidence to share your knowledge, and the situational awareness to protect yourself and your followers. This book is not going to show you how to set up a business or help you find your passion. This book will help you create a space where your business and your passion can connect with more people than you ever imagined.

When my message and my first book was ready for the masses, I researched what had worked for others and I followed all the advice I could find. I was following in the footsteps of those who had gone before me and hoping I would stumble upon the same success. Copying what had worked for other people, most of whom had more experience and a bigger audience, did not work for me, however. Through the trying and failing, I discovered a way to quickly grow a tribe of invested and engaged followers. I can't say this system is easy in the sense that it is effortless, because it is not. Growing a flock of followers will take work, attention, and dedication. It will take knowledge and patience. It will require a thick skin. If you truly believe the same way I do, that your message matters and can change lives, then the climbing and falling will be worth it and knowing your success is the result of your hard work will make the victory that much sweeter.

My first Facebook group, Flight Attendant Career Connection, has over 17,000 members. It has been featured in the Huffington Post, Yahoo Travel, Mashable.com and even by Facebook itself. The thing that makes the group special is the encouraging group of people who are members. The thing that makes the business successful is my dedication to those people.

Using a Facebook group marketing plan, or any marketing plan for that matter, isn't a magic tunnel to success. It is a path to success: an uneven, poorly marked, danger at every turn, path. Again, this quest to run and market a small business in not effortless, but the basics are pretty simple. Build relationships through generosity. Convert customers by offering amazing value. Create fame that will open any door you want to walk through.

So, What's Up With Facebook?

You don't have to be a marketing professional to know how much influence online communities have over what we read, buy, and even believe. Social media marketing is a must for anyone looking to sell anything online or at a physical location. What did you do the last time you wanted an opinion on anything from what book you should read on vacation, to when you should plant your tomatoes, to the cause of the strange rash all over your six-year-old's back? You asked social media. You posted on Facebook. You sent out a tweet. You searched Pinterest. When faced with a problem, we no longer immediately consult an expert. First, we ask our Facebook friends, then we seek out an expert as a second opinion. This is why organizing a group of dedicated followers on a social media platform is so important. Even after you establish yourself as the expert, most people will not come straight to you with their problem or question. They will ask their peers within the tribe. Let your tribe direct the question asker to you, and you will have even more influence. A recommendation will trump self-promotion any day of the week. Whether you are selling books, ideas, songs, or widgets, without a presence on social media, you are missing a huge opportunity to make a difference and claim your share of the market.

It is not hard to find advice, both good and bad, regarding social media. Everyone has a theory and a tip for your business, but the sheer volume of information can lead to confusion. When it comes to social media, the options are almost endless. Twitter, Pinterest, Facebook, Instagram, Tumblr, LinkedIn, the list goes on and is changing and growing every day. I mean, first you had to be on Facebook. Then they changed the algorithm they use to decide which newsfeed any given post will appear and started charging money to increase post visibility. Some people jumped off the Facebook ship when this happened.

What about Twitter? The life of a tweet is only about 10 seconds, so that's a tough hurdle to overcome. Plus, you are limited to 140 characters. Personally, I have too much to say to be limited all the time.

What about Pinterest? The current social media experts encourage you to turn all your blog posts and web pages into a pin and start pinning away. But Pinterest moves pretty quickly, and unless you have a graphic eye, your pins are going to stink. Stinky pins don't get shared.

All these options, coupled with the knock your socks off success stories that emerge from every platform, left me scattered, frustrated, and confused. You may feel the same way and find yourself asking the question, "Where should I be active: Facebook, Pinterest, LinkedIn, Instagram, Twitter, Tumblr, Tribrr, Ello or Google+?"

YES! The answer to that question is, "Yes." You should have a complete profile with a link to your website and pictures of you or your logo on every one of these sites. You should even visit each site from time to time to comment, update your profile, and perform general housekeeping duties. That being said, you do not have to be "active" on every form of social media. Honestly, you only need an engaged group of followers, or a tribe, on one platform.

The platform I chose was Facebook. I like Facebook for several reasons. One of the best things about choosing to build your tribe on Facebook is the barrier to entry is extremely low. A Facebook account is free. A business page on Facebook is free. Creating a group on Facebook is free. And all of these are easily managed not only from a computer but right from your phone. Whenever I have a few spare minutes, I scroll through my Facebook notifications, accept new members into my group, and "like" a couple of posts. I usually even have time to comment on several questions. This is mostly done with one hand because at this time in my life my other hand is almost always holding a baby. I am in constant contact with my entire tribe without having to sit down at the computer and answer emails or write an entire blog post. As easy as it is for me to access my tribe, it is just as easy for my members to access me. They are never left searching for an email address to contact me. Facebook makes it so easy to message me or tag me in a post.

Another benefit of Facebook is it is so user friendly. You can create a profile, a page, or a group quickly and easily. There is no certification or validation needed to establish yourself as a business or brand. Answer a few questions, upload a few photos and you are open for business.

Thirdly, pretty much everyone is on Facebook. Everyone from your grandma to your middle-schooler has a Facebook account and most people enjoy spending a little time on Facebook every day. Facebook has done an amazing job of creating an app that is extremely easy to use. I have already talked about how invaluable having Facebook on my phone is to my business. With over a million people using Facebook from their mobile phones, you have access to your customer's eyes almost constantly.

Another reason I love Facebook for tribe building is the option to make Facebook posts that are text only, graphic only, or a combination of both. Based on research, pictures and graphics together tend to have a further reach on Facebook, but text only posts can do quite well if the content is valuable, interesting, or funny. With no character limit, I can pop in for a quick update, or I can offer valuable content that is several paragraphs long.

I have found tremendous success using Facebook to collect and connect with my followers. It hasn't always been easy. I have dealt with ups and downs and even a hater or two, but in the end, I am connecting with people I am passionate about serving and I am making more money than I ever imagined. You can find the same success I have by learning from my triumphs and setbacks. Hold on tight, because I'm about to show you everything you need to begin making money with Facebook groups.

☐

Facebook Royalty

The original goal of my Facebook group, Flight Attendant Career Connection, was to support the sale of my first book, <u>Looking Skyward: Turn Your Flight Attendant Dreams Into Reality</u>. I started out with the idea that I would have a secret group and giveaway memberships as an incentive to buy Looking Skyward. Although other authors have found success with this idea, using the group as a free gift with purchase did not work for me. I had no platform or influence in the niche I was targeting. I had no way to get the word about my book and the group out to my potential readers. My book sales started out slowly and my group sat stagnant with only seven members for a few months. I had three people buy the book and join the group organically, but for four months, I saw no real growth or action. One day I got fed up with my little group and its twelve members. There was not enough traffic for the group to provide any real value and it was not serving its purpose. This frustration gave me a surge of confidence to do more and I realized I had to do something if I wanted this group to offer any help or encouragement to anyone. From my own flight attendant job search, I knew the forums on the job search website Indeed.com were extremely active with my target audience, which is aspiring flight attendants. I copied the link to my group and posted it on the forum with a little note that said something to the effect of, "Have y'all seen this new group on FB? Looks pretty good." Then I waited. It wasn't long before a few requests to join Flight Attendant Career Connection showed up in my notifications. It was working and I was thrilled.

Even though I only shared the link to my group a few times on the website outside of Facebook, the momentum those few links created never slowed down. It took about two and half months to reach 1,000 members. After that first 1,000, the group began to grow steadily by about 75 members a week, then 100 members a week. The second 1,000 members took about eleven weeks to gain. Flight Attendant Career Connection has been averaging about 1,000 new members a month ever since and we have recently surpassed 17,000 members.

When I started Flight Attendant Career Connection, all I had for sale was a book. As the group began to grow, I began to receive requests for coaching and individual sessions. When my group was about five months old, I formalized and monetized my coaching program and the company Flight Attendant Career Connection was born. I now offer coaching, resume rewrites, a book, and an interview workbook. I've even hosted a live workshop that had a corporate sponsor. Every one of my customers come to me through either word of mouth or the Facebook group. Although I now pay Facebook to boost posts from time to time, I started with zero advertising budget and I have doubled my family's monthly income with my work from home business.

Once we passed 5,000 members, Facebook itself took notice. I was contacted by Brittany, a Facebook employee who was impressed by not only my numbers but the community I had built. Flight Attendant Career Connection was featured in Facebook Stories. Facebook even sent a camera crew to my house to film a special interview for Mark Zuckerberg. This opportunity became a wave of media exposure including podcast interviews, blog mentions, and even interviews for Mashable.com, Yahoo Travel, and the Huffington Post articles.

Nine thousand is a big number. Although numbers aren't everything, I am not going to sit here and tell you numbers don't matter. When I first started blogging, I remember hearing successful bloggers say they didn't think the number of followers and page views they had was very important. They would write about sharing from the heart and letting the process of creating something beautiful be the only thing that mattered. I think that's easy to say when you have reached the level of success that comes from thousands of followers and you are fully supporting your family by selling advertising in the sidebar of your blog. Even though I understand where they are coming from, I doubt they report back to their advertisers with statistics on how honest and creative they had been on their blog that month. Numbers do matter.

The importance of numbers is in the way your group is perceived. When people see a lot of people hanging out in one place, they equate that with value. Bars and nightclubs have used this natural human reaction as a marketing tool for years. Have you ever noticed that the hottest club in town always has a line? Have you ever waited in that line? Odds are, the line made the club popular, not the other way around. Bouncers are encouraged to keep the sidewalk full to give the perception of value. Is the hot club really that much better than the club next door with no line? Maybe. Maybe not. But it sure looks like it is a better place to see and be seen. As your Facebook group begins to grow, it will grow slowly at first. You'll add just a few new members at a time and then you'll add a few more and a few more until you are adding fifteen new members at a time, several times a day. You should be growing. Things that are healthy grow. Children. Plants. Facebook groups.

Large numbers and the perception of value will matter if you decide to partner with other businesses. Whether you ask for sponsors or sell advertising space on your website, once you start to collect advertising money, the numbers will matter. If your following is growing, you must be doing something right to cause all those people to want to hang out on your little piece of the internet and listen to what you have to say. Big numbers can also lead to sponsors, expert status, and sales. As your tribe grows, so do your opportunities.

What numbers don't do is define your worth as a person, writer, or entrepreneur. When I say numbers matter, I mean they are a great way to measure whether or not you are on the right track and heading in the right direction. If you put too much effort into recruiting everyone to join you, you will fail twice. First, you will fail because you will never be able to make everyone join your group. That's impossible. Second, you will fail because you will be spending too much time chasing the ones that are not in the group and not enough time with those who have joined you. Failing the members you already have is the worst thing you can do. Be careful you do not expend so much time or energy trying to reach your future readers that you run out of time and energy for your current readers. Spend most, if not all, of your resource providing value to the ones who have already signed up to follow you. Give them all you've got and you will naturally create the best advertising campaign possible: word of mouth referrals.

I have had a lot of success using Facebook to grow an engaged tribe of followers. I know social media and Facebook is constantly changing. I also know that I don't own the platform and if Facebook changes the rules of the game, my successful group of faithful followers could be gone tomorrow. I've read all the warnings and I've listened to all the experts when they tell me building a tribe only on social media is risky. I've read the reports and the blog posts that came out after the last Facebook algorithm change and I know the disappointment that came with it. Having your reach cut in half or even quartered can be frustrating and if you convert most of your paying clients from Facebook, a change in your reach can be downright scary.

Because I understand all the dangers involved with building a tribe on a platform owned by someone else, I'm hedging against that risk by constantly collecting email addresses. My Facebook group grew very quickly and it continues to grow at a pretty quick rate, so keeping up with the collection of email addresses is something I have to do on purpose. My email list lives over at MailChimp. I use it to send out a newsletter or email when I have something exciting to announce. I make sure I contact my email list at least once a month. I do not use my email list as the primary means of communication with my tribe. I do not send out important information in an email without posting it to the Facebook group, too. I use the email to support the relationships I build on Facebook.

Growing a tribe that is engaged with you and each other boils down to one thing: relationship. It really is all about developing strong, healthy relationships with the group of people you want to influence. Building relationship takes work and action. These online or business relationships aren't any different from other relationships you decide are important enough to nurture. Whether it's a friendship, a family relationship, or a marriage, the choices you make and the work you put in will determine the outcome and the strength of the connection.

You may be wondering what steps you should take to build relationships inside your Facebook group. The answer is, "The same way you build a relationship with your children or your spouse."

Show up and act interested.
Listen to stories.
Be quick with encouragement and a positive word.
Always tell the truth and build trust.
Forgive when the comments sting.
Give grace when obligations are ignored.

Online business relationships work the same way. Set the foundation of your group on these basic building blocks and you will form a strong alliance with the members of your group. Trust me when I tell you it's scary out there. You're going to need all the allies you can get.

Before we get into the how-to of building a Facebook group, I want to talk about the what. What is the reason it is so important for you, your brand, or your business to have an engaged group of followers? What is the benefit of collecting your customers and clients together in one place? The answer: Community is Powerful! Societies have banded together with common interests, beliefs, and goals since time began which proves there must be some value in establishing a community of followers. These communities are called many things: congregations, towns, villages, communes, but the best term to define these groups is a tribe. In his book Tribes, Seth Godin defines the term tribe by saying, "A tribe is a group of people connected to one another, connected to a leader, and connected to an idea. For millions of years, human beings have been part of one tribe or another. A group needs only two things to be a tribe: a shared interest and a way to communicate."

Like I said before, I am not going to tell you numbers don't matter. I believe they matter a lot, but they don't matter in the way you may think. Looking at the number of members you have in your group is an awful way to define success. Numbers are infinite, so there will always, always, always be people out there who are not in your group, not buying your product, or not reading your material. Odds are, there will always be someone who has more readers than you.

The best way to measure the effectiveness or the success of your Facebook group is by looking at engagement. Are your followers showing up every day, asking questions, and interacting with each other, or do you log in and hear crickets chirping? When you first begin to grow your Facebook group and engage your tribe you will start most of the conversations. To increase engagement, you must post a question or an inspirational quote every day. Some days, your post might go completely ignored or receive a few mercy "likes", but you have to keep offering opportunities for your tribe to engage with you and with each other. You do not have to ask a question that is completely on the topic of your group every time you post. The goal is just to get them talking. Talking and learning about one another builds relationships and relationships lead to sales.

These relationships can be built anywhere: in the comments of a blog, over a fence in your front yard, or on social media, but I don't think any social media platform encourages relationship building as well as Facebook. Facebook has been the leader in social media marketing and they continue to lead. Even with the recent changes for business users, no one does social media communities better than Facebook.

☐

Round 'Um Up on Facebook

I think it's about time we got down to the nitty-gritty of Facebook group building. Are you on Facebook? Mostly likely, the answer is, "Yes." If you are not on Facebook and you want to sell anything to anyone, you absolutely have to be on Facebook. The level of activity is up to you, but you need to be there. Yes, anyone can see what you post, but that does not change the fact that you still have complete control over what you post. You are responsible for creating the boundaries with which you are comfortable. You don't have to post pictures of your children, or tell the world your address if that makes you uncomfortable. In fact, you could make it a place you talk strictly about yourself and your business, book, or project.

There are three places you can be active on Facebook. I encourage you to be active in all three. The first thing you need is a profile. You will automatically set one up the first time you log into Facebook. Your profile needs to have your name and your picture. I use my profile the same way most people around the world use a Facebook page. I post pictures of my kids, my dinner, and anything else I find interesting. I complain about the traffic, I wish old school mates Happy Birthday, and I ask for help when I need a problem solved. Remember, you decide what you are comfortable posting about your life, but you need to post something.

The next step in setting yourself up for Facebook success is creating a Facebook page. Facebook pages, sometimes called "Like Pages" or "Fan Pages" are designed to be a sort of profile for your business or your brand. Use your page like a billboard. Announce new products or share about an exciting change. You will not have much interaction on your page. You will get likes and comments, but your customers cannot easily interact with you or each other because you are the only one starting conversations. If they don't have anything to say about your choice of subject, they will remain silent. I have two Facebook pages. One for Flight Attendant Career Connection and one titled Abbie Unger: Coach, Travel, Speak. I will announce this book over at Flight Attendant Career Connection, but most of the book updates will be posted on my author page, Abbie Unger: Coach, Travel, Speak. The ability to have more than one Facebook page is perfect for multi-passionate entrepreneurs like me.

Your Facebook page is where Facebook makes money off of you.

Having a page is free, but your posts will not automatically be shown to all of your followers. Facebook has a special algorithm that they use to decide what is displayed in any given newsfeed. They take into consideration where you have liked, commented, or shared in the past and they try to predict what you would like to see in the future. As the owner of the page, you can pay Facebook or "boost" your posts to make it visible to more people. I think it is more than fair for Facebook to charge a small fee to help you advertise. Once you decide to boost a post, you are in control of the amount of money you want to invest and the target demographic you want to reach. For as little as a dollar, you can get your ad in front of hundreds of targeted customers. I think that's a pretty good deal. You can also increase the reach of your post by posting something that is so interesting or valuable that your followers begin to comment and share. As your followers share the post, it will show up on more Facebook newsfeeds. Once Facebook recognizes the popularity of your post it will begin to show the post to more of your followers. My Facebook page, Flight Attendant Career Connection, has just under 700 "likes" (remember, my group has over 9,000, not my page) but last week, I had a post go viral. As of this writing, that post has been viewed 31,280 times because it was shared 327 times. These numbers happened without boosting, or paying Facebook to show the post to more people, but organically.

Be strategic about what you post to your page. Do not share anything from inside the group that is private. For example, when my clients announce in the group they hit their goal and received a job offer to become a flight attendant, we celebrate, but I never share that information on the page unless I have permission. The page is public and they may not have told their employer yet. Be mindful of this because the internet makes the world a lot smaller than you would imagine. Use your page to announce specials and share inspirations or current events that are relevant. It will take a bit of trial and error to discover what your customers enjoy reading and more importantly, sharing. Although you will be more active in your group, posting to your page about once a day is plenty, just don't limit yourself. If you have more to say, say it. Don't stress yourself out attempting to create content for the page. The good stuff happens inside the group.

Now for the Fun: Facebook Groups

My group, Flight Attendant Career Connection, is where I have built all my business relationships, converted my customers, and found fame. If you have a business or brand, you have got to start a Facebook group today. They are easy and free to create. The steps for setting up a group are similar to the steps for creating a page, but you don't have to answer nearly as many questions. There are only a few things to consider as you set up your group: name, privacy setting, and description.

The name of your group should make it easy for people to know what's happening behind the privacy wall. The name of your group may be different from the name of your book or your business. The title of my first book is Looking Skyward, but that is not the name of my group. If I had named my group Looking Skyward, it would have been difficult for my target audience to find me. What does Looking Skyward mean anyway? Is it a place for bird watchers, cloud shape enthusiasts, or religious zealots waiting for the return of Christ? Instead, I chose a name that is self-explanatory: Flight Attendant Career Connection. My business came about because of my group, so they do share the same name.

Here are a few more examples:

Corie Clark has an awesome book titled The Simplicity Project. This book teaches the importance of living a life that is free from clutter and chaos. She walks readers through the steps needed to live a life of peace and purpose. The name of her first Facebook group is The Simplicity Project. She was able to name her Facebook group after her book because the title clearly defines what the group is all about. Her book doesn't need the subtitle like mine does. As her business has continued to grow, Corie has created more products to help people live a purposeful life. Her Purposeful Planner has been wildly successful. The excitement inspired her to create another group called The Purposeful Planner for fans and owners of her beautiful planner. In this group, members share pictures of their planners complete with color coding systems, stickers, and washi tape.

Matt Ham originally named his Facebook group The Live Richly Community. He is passionate about helping people redefine what a wealthy life looks like. His book, <u>Redefine Rich</u> is showing people how they can live a life that is truly rich. He did not use the title of his book as the name of his group either, but the branding is consistent enough to tie the two together. Adding the word Community was a nice touch. His brand has evolved and Matt recently changed the name of the group to The Whole Life Community.

Kelsey Humphreys' book is titled <u>GO SOLO: How to Quit the Job You Hate and Start a Small Business You Love</u> and the name of her group is GO SOLO: Tools, Inspiration and Support for Solopreneurs. Kelsey used a hybrid of the title of the book and the purpose of the group. She created her group and offered community and resources to her readers before the book was released. There is no need to wait until after you have something to sell. Start building relationships and creating fame right now using a Facebook group. Kelsey is now the host of a traveling interview show called The Pursuit. Can you guess what she changed the name of her group to? That's right, The Pursuit Community.

After you chose a name, the next step to set up a Facebook group is to choose a privacy setting. I recommend you choose to make your group "closed." This means the name of the group and the names of the members of the group will be visible to everyone, but not the actual posts inside the group. Your group will show up in the search results and anyone can request to join. Every new member will need to be approved by an administrator, but they will not need to be invited by a current member to request to join. The other options for privacy settings are "public" or "private." If you chose public, posts made inside the group will show up in the news feeds of people who are not members of the group. I run a career site and my members do not want their questions to be public because their current employer may not be aware of their new career aspirations. Even if you do not foresee a problem like this, I still recommend a closed group. This gives your members the freedom to ask questions that they may not want splashed all over Facebook.

On the other hand, a private group is too hidden. The name of your group will not show up in the search results and new members will need to be invited by a current member. They cannot request to join on their own. It will be impossible for a group with a private setting to grow organically.

The third and final step before you set up your Facebook group is to define the purpose of your group and write a clear description. Because your group is closed and anyone will be able to see your description, use the same principles you used to name your group to clearly explain the purpose of your group. Include who is welcome in your group, and what your member's can expect to find inside the group. Include a link to your website and your email address. You can also highlight any products or services you offer. I have a few testimonials in my description, too.

You will also need to include a rule or two. Make it clear in the description that everyone is welcome, but the admin reserves the right to delete any posts or comments and members may be removed at the discretion of the admin. Make sure your rules do not come across as rude. Because the group description may be your first introduction to some people, make sure your rules don't overshadow your value. The rules don't even need to be prominent or strong. Just add a tiny sentence at the bottom of your description. We will talk more about what to watch for and how to handle disruptions and spam a little later in this book. For now, just make sure your description is clear and inviting. At the bottom of the description, Facebook will let you assign three keywords or "tag" the group. These tags help Facebook know to whom they should suggest your group based on their interests. Finally, add a picture and you're all set. Here is my description for Flight Attendant Career Connection:

"This is a community of dreamers and flyers. Here you will find tips, insider tricks, new job postings and general encouragement to help you down the path to earning your flight attendant wings. Because airlines hire in groups, we aren't competing against each other, but we are competing with each other. Ask a question, vent or offer advice. Your dream to become a flight attendant is attainable!

This group is a free resource provided by the company, Flight Attendant Career Connection.

For a full list of services visit:

Disclosure: Some of the products suggested in the group are affiliate links, which means FACC receives a commission from the sale of these items.

Coaching sessions with Abbie Unger, are live and face to face using Skype or Facetime. Coaching is an incredibly valuable tool. Answering interview questions for the first time while sitting in the hot seat in front of a recruiter is a bad idea and could cost. Let's work together to craft your stories using the STAR format to achieve the clarity you need to successfully present your skills, experience, and personality.

"I can attest to that as well. I hadn't had ANY job interview in 13 years, much less an FA interview, and I landed the CJO on the first try! Abbie's coaching is definitely advantageous and so worth the minimal fee - you won't regret it!"~Laura, ExpressJet

"I got my cjo after having 2 sessions with Abbie Unger. I don't think I would have have gotten it otherwise. Had already been turned down a few times. I knew I was qualified and Abbie showed me how to present myself better. It was a tiny amt. of money invested to get the desired results. Try it!" ~Valerie, Spirit Airline

FACC Interview Workbook:
$20.00 for the PDF download (you can print the workbook out from your home printer)
This workbook is treasure maps designed to guide and direct you to your dreams come true. I explain interview strategies and the STAR interview method in clear and easy to understand terms. This workbook includes over 50 real airline interview questions and space for you to write out and perfect your answers. The book is divided into four sections: personality questions, STAR format questions, onboard situation questions, and "tell me what you think" questions. I've also included a mock announcement for you to practice reading aloud. This book does not contain any answers, but will assist you as you discover what you want to say during your interview.

Abbie Unger's first eBook, <u>Looking Skyward: Turn Your Flight Attendant Dreams Into Reality</u>, is an in-depth guide to becoming a flight attendant. The book is available online.

The admin has the right to remove any posts or comments she considers inappropriate.

Please do not post ads for products, services, or non-airlines jobs without first contacting Abbie Unger. Thanks!"

Here are the step by step instructions to set up a new Facebook group:

1) Log into your personal Facebook account.

2) Scroll down until you see the word "Groups" on the left side of the screen. Click on the words "Create Group" and wait for the box to pop up.

3) Fill in the box with the name you have chosen for your group. Facebook requires you to add at least one person. Do not go spamming your entire friend list by adding them to the group. Add one person you know will not mind. Someone like your husband or your mom. They can always leave the group later or turn off the notifications.

4) Click the box next to the words, "Add this group to your favorites." This will make accessing the group easier the next time you log in.

5) Choose your privacy setting. The default is "closed" which is the setting I recommend for most groups.

6) Click "Create."

7) Choose a graphic from those provided by Facebook. You could skip this step, but why would you? Once you have chosen your picture, click "OK."

Congratulations! You just created a new group. Now you need to dress it up with a cover photo, add your description, and begin to invite members.

BUILD RELATIONSHIPS

All Relationships are the Same

Now that you have your group named, your privacy setting set, and your description posted, you're ready to start building relationships. The very best way to sell anything is through relationships. Remember what I said you need to do to build relationships?

Show up and act interested.

Listen to stories.

Be quick with encouragement and a positive word.

Always tell the truth and build trust.

Forgive when the comments sting.

Give grace when obligations are ignored.

People buy products from those they know, like, and trust. The more you interact and serve, the more customers you will have. And the more customers you have, the more you will sell.

If you are consistently building relationships and connections with your members, you will be converting customers and creating fame before you know it.

Give it Away, Give it Away, Give it Away, Now

Generosity is the first step in building relationships. When you initially start out building a business, it is hard to give things away. Your resources are limited, the number of products you have to offer is limited and your capital is limited. I know it sounds counterintuitive, but if you want to be successful and you want to be successful quickly, you have got to be generous. Before you get scared know this, to be generous, you don't have to give away the farm. Generosity is not defined by how much you give away or how much you charge for your products and services. Generosity is an attitude. Generosity builds trust. Trust builds relationships. And relationships build successful businesses.

Everyone loves to receive gifts. Gift giving is one of the most demonstrative ways we celebrate each other. We exchange Birthday presents, Christmas presents, and Anniversary presents to honor each other and the relationships we share. Even though you won't be exchanging birthday gifts with the members of your group, there are plenty of generous gifts you can give. Corie gave her group a tangible gift. For three days, she offered a coupon code for a discount when they purchased her book, The Simplicity Project. This coupon code was only advertised inside her group as a way to thank the insiders for being a part of her community. Not only did her members appreciate her generosity, she also saw a spike in book sales. Corie's coupon code was a great idea, but not every gift has to be as tangible as a coupon.

Give the Gift of Time

The time you spend in your group is a gift to your members. Commenting and liking their posts takes time. Asking open-ended questions and engaging in conversations, even if they are off-topic and will never result in a sale, takes time and builds the relationship. Reading and filtering through articles and news stories and sharing the ones that your members will find interesting takes time. Another way to offer your time is by responding to Facebook messages and emails, especially as you are growing. Think about how you would feel if you received a personalized email answer from someone you respected. Pretty special, huh? You may get to the point where you have to systemize and change your policies on answering emails, but when you are in the building stages, answer every one.

Facebook will notify you when you receive a message from someone you are Facebook friends with or someone you have had a lot of interaction within the group. If a new member who you have not yet connected with sends you a message, it may end up in your "other" folder. You can find the tab for your other folder right next to the inbox tab in your message box. Don't forget to check your other folder every day. You do not want to miss an opportunity. Create a new email address using the name of your group and make that address public. This will help you organize where your emails are coming from. Just don't forget to check your new email address every day, too.

Give the Gift of Answers

Let's face it, most people will join your group because they have a problem and it looks like the answer might be found inside the group. Whether that is a career problem, a lifestyle problem, or just an "I can't find anyone with the same crazy interest as me problem", your group will offer the solution. Because you are the grand supreme ruler of the Facebook group, you will be asked a lot of questions. Even though the answer to these questions can also be found in your book or during a coaching session, be generous with your expertise. When you are asked a question, you don't have to give away every secret, trick, and piece of advice you have in your arsenal but do remember you are building relationships and inspiring others to have confidence in your expertise. Answer the question! You can add a blurb explaining that more information can be found on your website or in your book, but that is only after you have sufficiently answered the original question. Never answer a question with only a link to your book or services page. If you are going to suggest they invest in what you are selling, please answer the question first. As your group grows, you will find yourself answering the same questions over and over again. This can feel like a waste of time but don't be tempted to "encourage" the question asker to scroll through the posts and find the answer.

Although I believe you should make sure every question gets an answer, there are a few ways you can make answering frequently asked questions easier. One option is to create a list of FAQ, save it under the files tab at the top of the group's "discussion" page, and direct people there to find answers. Another idea is to use these questions as inspiration for blog posts, YouTube videos, or better yet, both. Once you have your blog posts written and your videos filmed, you can save so much time, while still delivering generous value, by sharing these posts instead of typing the same answers out over and over again. Sending a potential customer to your website is always a good idea. Once they are on your site, you have a better chance of capturing their email address and they will be exposed to the products and services you sell. Some potential customers won't even know you are a business, not just a Facebook group until they visit your website. Directing potential customers to the place where they can learn about you and all you have to offer a great idea.

YouTube is the second largest search engine behind Google. Create a new video for each of the recurring questions you receive in your Facebook group. Odds are, if your members are asking these questions, then your not-yet-members are probably typing the same questions into a search engine somewhere. Because you will have followers and non-followers watching your public YouTube videos, make sure you quickly introduce yourself at the beginning of each video and invite new viewers to join your Facebook group. Include a clickable link in the video description to make joining your Facebook group even easier.

I use both blog posts and YouTube videos to answer questions in my group. I frequently receive questions regarding what to wear to an interview, what should be included in a flight attendant resume, and what to expect when attending a face to face interview, but the number one question I receive is, "How can I do well on the video interview?" More and more airlines are using a video interview to narrow down the number of candidates they invite to a live interview. These video interviews are stressful and a new experience for most of my Facebook group members. I created a funny and informative video to offer advice and relive a bit of the stage fright. Now, whenever that question comes up, I have an easy way answer.

Every time someone asks you to answer a question, consider it an honor that they value your expertise so much. Be respectful and don't scold the question asker for not doing enough research before they asked the question. So in case you missed it, I want you to answer the question.

Give the Gift of Encouragement

The world is a bad, scary place. It is full of disappointment and heartache. There is always someone ready and willing to tell your members why whatever it is they are dreaming of is never going to become a reality. If you can make your little piece of the internet, your Facebook group, a place where the encouragement flows, people will not only visit, they will move in, take up residence and become your most valuable marketing tool. The value of a simple, "Good job!" or "You got this!" became clear to me when one of my group members posted a heartfelt thank you for the encouragement she had found in Flight Attendant Career Connection. She posted that Flight Attendant Career Connection was the only place she could go where people understood her dream and encouraged her to go for it. Everyone else in her life was quick to tell her why becoming a flight attendant was a silly dream. Did you catch that? All the people in her life think her dream is silly. Posts like this one make me sad because they show how many people in the world are surrounded by nothing but negativity. I'm proud of the encouragement I give and the spirit of camaraderie I facilitate in my Facebook group. Everyone is looking for a safe place to tell their story. If you have all the answers to all the questions, people will visit you when they face a problem. If you make them feel good while they are here, they will stay.

☐

Grow Your Group

Your group should grow naturally and organically as you engage with your members and your members engage with each other. The value your group provides will cause members to want to invite their friends and those friends invite more friends and then Facebook begins to suggest your group to non-members based on their interests. Once this happens you are on the road to big numbers, big relationships, and big success. I jumpstarted the growth of my group by talking about it in other forums. This worked for me, but I was very careful and very strategic. When posting in someone else's space, there is a fine line between promoting and spamming.

If your group is shrinking or the growth has stalled considerably, then you are not running a healthy group. Again, things that are healthy, children, plants, Facebook groups, grow. Are you encouraging your members? Are you "liking" every post and commenting? Are you answering questions? Maybe you're not growing because you are not investing enough time connecting and being visible in your group. Take a look at where your energy has been focused and find a new way to offer something valuable to your members. Are you in the middle of a book edit? Offer your members a sneak peak or a free chapter. Are your kids home for the summer? Post a fun picture every now and then. Has your workload and client list increased? Schedule time to answer questions and comment on Facebook posts. Consider setting up "office hours." Pick an hour or two a week that you can spend on Facebook answering questions live.

At least once a day, post an interesting question for your members to answer or start an interesting conversation. Here are a few questions to help you get those juices flowing.

- Where is everyone today?
- What steps are you taking this week to move you toward your goals?
- I just finished an amazing book and now I'm looking for a fun beach   read/inspiring business book/exciting thriller. What's your favorite?
- Let's all share a picture of our families. I'll go first.
- What's your favorite song right now? I'm loving this one…….
- Don't forget this is a place for questions. If you have a burning

one, I want to hear it.

- Where is your favorite place to visit?

As your group grows, you will have more people talking about your group and inviting friends to join. As your group becomes more and more active, Facebook will begin to suggest the group to people who have interests matching your group tags. This is called the "snowball effect." The more activity in your group, the bigger your snowball. The bigger your snowball, the bigger your impact.

Protect and Serve

As the administrator of the Facebook group, you are also the protector. As people join your group, connect with your brand and business, and begin to trust, you will owe it to them to do your best to protect them. You will protect your members from spam, inaccurate information, and you will even protect your members from each other.

SPAM

As soon as you have more than twelve members, you will begin to see spammy ads, usually for Oakley Sunglasses, in your Facebook group. After a while, you won't pay any attention to these ads, but at the beginning of your growth curve these spammy ads will send you on a rollercoaster of frustration. First, you will receive a notification that someone besides you finally posted in your group. With great excitement you will check out the post, but the excitement will quickly turn to disappointment when you discover the post is nothing but a picture selling something that you aren't buying. The ad is easy enough to delete, but then you are faced with the choice. Delete the member who spammed your board or only delete the post and let them stay to spam another day. I know when you are reading this, and when I put it like that, the obvious choice is to delete the member and ban them from your group but when you are still small and growing slowly, it is easy to feel like deleting any member is the last thing you want to do. I understand that and I'm not going to tell you that you have to delete every sneaky spammer that crosses your path but in the end, you are going to delete them. Your group will eventually have enough members that the one or two sneaky spammers won't affect your numbers at all. Most of these accounts are fake accounts which means there is no one on the other end who might get their feeling hurts. So in the beginning, it's up to you. Let them stay or make them go. In the end it won't matter either way.

Now that I've told you about the sneaky spammer, let's talk a little bit about the accidental spammer. This is the person who does not realize your group is actually part of the marketing plan for your business. They think the tribe you have painstakingly built is just an accidental space of wonderment on the internet. They see what they believe is an opportunity and they seize it. These ads can show up in several different ways. Most often, you will see them as a post on your board. You will know this isn't the work of a sneaky spammer because the post will include more than just a picture of a product with a link. It will include some sort of introduction or description of the product or service offered. The accidental spammer will try to do exactly what you are doing, build a relationship with potential customers. I see this a lot from people who are involved in multilevel marketing. I respect and admire their hustle, but I still don't let them sell from my platform. Remember your platform, or your Facebook group in this instance, is just that. It's yours. Do not let just anyone climb up there and stand beside you.

When you stumble upon these accidental spammers, you have a couple of options. You can simply delete the post. When you are deleting a post that was obviously put there by a real person who is trying to grow a real business, do them a favor and send them a message. You want to let them know that their post was deleted on purpose so they don't think it disappeared into cyberspace and needs to be re-posted. You also want to open the lines of communication. They already think you control a space of the internet where they would like to have their business highlighted, so why not use this as a chance to partner together. If you want to monetize your platform through paid advertising, offer a blog post and access to your Facebook group for a fee. The partnership does not have to be a financial transaction. It is totally fine to let people post or talk about their business on your board without charging them, but that needs to be a decision that you make on purpose. Never let anyone advertise another business on your page without first talking to you. You have to be the gatekeeper and protector of your group. Respect their trust and vet everything before it is presented to your followers.

Another way a legitimate business may spam your followers is by sending them personal messages on Facebook. I have to be honest, I think this is way out of line and it feels to me like a way to avoid the administrator of a group. Most of them are smart enough not to send the administrator the spammy message so you will find out about these messages when one member sends you a message asking if you know anything about the ad they received from another member or when your mom sends you a text message asking you about the multilevel travel opportunity she was offered because she was a member of Flight Attendant Career Connection. As crazy as that text was, nothing is quite as bad as waking up to a message from one of your faithful members asking if you are aware that your direct competition is sending private messages to all your members.

When I find out someone is sending messages to my members, I always message them right away and ask them to stop. I feel like an advertising Facebook message is intrusive and I do not allow even my sponsors to cold message my members. I will include ads or information from time to time in my emails, but never in a Facebook message. Even though I am very clear about my desire for them to stop messaging my members, I am always careful to make any contact I have professional and respectful. I am a big believer in giving the benefit of the doubt and never burning any bridges. Plus, you never know where a relationship might lead.

Relationship is the foundation of success. Relationship is what connects you to your customers and relationship is what makes others want to learn more about you. If you live your life and run your business with a generous spirit and look out for those who are supporting you, you can't lose. Good, healthy relationships are what makes converting customer and creating fame possible.

CONVERT CUSTOMERS

Show Me the Money

Now that you know how to find and engage the members of your group, it is time to start talking about converting them to customers. Building a large platform is rewarding, but if you are anything like me, you're thinking, "Show me the money!" Converting interested browsers into paying customers is a challenge for every business owner. Whether they are internet marketers, buying TV ads, or paying someone to stand on the side of the road dressed like a chicken, the goal is the same: convert lookers into buyers.

Having your own Facebook group full of people who are passionate or interested in the thing you are selling is a great start. You have corralled your target audience into one space and you can talk to them about your books, products, or services without paying for advertising. That my friend, is a pretty sweet deal. But it is not going to work if you are not strategic about the way you go about converting customers. First, you will need to establish yourself as an authority. You become an authority by sharing your knowledge and being authentic. The next step in converting customers is advertising without spamming. You could have a million members in your Facebook group, but if they don't know what you're selling, they won't be buying. Don't forget to collect email addresses and direct customers to an easy to use website and you will be well on your way to making money with your Facebook group.

Be Knowledgeable

A few years ago, I attended my first blogger conference. I had been blogging less than a year at that point, but I had found my voice and built up a tiny but faithful little group of readers. I was so excited to sit at the feet of bloggers who were miles ahead of me on the road to blogger success. I was ready to learn what they had done and how they had done it. I bought a ticket to the conference and sacrificed to make the hotel and food budget work. I invested in the expertise of the speakers. I cannot even tell you how many times I heard a speaker at this conference say, "I don't know why I'm up here. I'm just a mom. Or an artist. Or a blogger." Hearing these speakers speak so lowly of themselves made me feel like a fool for investing money to hear them speak. Even though I learned a lot at that conference and I believe every one of those speakers absolutely deserved to be speaking that weekend, their attempt at humility left me feeling disappointed about my choice to invest. When you pay money to learn from someone, the last thing you want to hear come out of their mouth is, "I don't know why you would want to learn from me." As your reputation as an expert grows, be careful you don't downplay your knowledge because you are uncomfortable. You earned your expertise, so own it.

You obviously feel like you have something to offer someone, right? I mean, why else would you set up shop and start offering your books or services to the world? You have the knowledge that sets you apart as an authority. Do not be afraid to own it. Talk about the things you have accomplished. Be proud of the difficulties you have overcome. Impart the knowledge you have gained through all the failures and successes you have endured. You can be proud and confident in what you know and what you have accomplished without being prideful and stuck up.

Even though I want you to be self-assured, be careful you don't let your confidence come across as cocky. No one likes a know-it-all. Finding the balance between approachable humility and proud expertise can be tough. Self-promote too much and you will turn people off to your message, but too much modesty can leave your followers hesitant to invest in what you're selling. This may take a little trial and error. There have been times I have posted something that I later felt was too spammy, so I deleted it. That's the beauty of

Facebook. Sure, some people probably saw it, but it didn't have to live forever and I learned from it. It won't be long before you discover the style and tone your followers respond to.

Being able to admit when you don't know something and then going out and finding the answer is part of being an expert. Occasionally you will be asked a question that you don't know the answer to. When this happens don't ignore the question and hope the post will get buried under the more active conversations. Don't make up an answer either. Let your member know you are not sure of the answer, but you will find out. Everyone will respect your ability to be honest even if it shows a place where you are lacking. You are the expert, but you are still a human. Seeing you say you aren't sure from time to time will cause your answers to have more authority. Everyone will know, if you say it, you're sure. As your group grows, so will your resources to answer questions. From time to time, you may be sent a message or an email containing a question you do not know the answer to off the top of your head. If I think this is a question that can be answered inside the Facebook group, I ask the question in the group. If it is appropriate, I'll tag the original question asker so they do not miss the answer. Using the resources available to you is the sign of a strong leader.

Being knowledgeable and staying knowledgeable are two different things. No matter what industry you are in, it is changing. Nothing ever stays the same and you need to stay out ahead of it. If you can be the first to talk about the happenings within the industry you will quickly establish yourself as an expert. You will answer a lot of questions as they come up in your tribe, but you also want to start a lot of the conversations, too. If you hear an interesting piece of news, share it in your group. If you learn something new, share that, too. This is true even if you are just sharing public news articles. Sure, everyone has access to news sites, but filtering through all the stories and sharing the ones that will be interesting to your group members is a service you can perform for your members. Don't forget to add a bit of a commentary to the "share" to spur on the conversation. The more conversation, the better.

Let your fail flag wave

Another way you can set yourself apart as an expert is by being transparent about your struggles. This one is hard, I'm not going to sugar coat it. It is scary and feels counterproductive to share your failures and your struggles as a way to prove your worth and ability to operate as an expert, but it works. The capacity to talk about your struggles and hardships on the way to making your dreams come true will inspire trust. No one thinks life is perfect or the road to success is straight. If you try to present your way as the guaranteed easy way, you will never gain a tribe of dedicated followers because no one will fully believe you. Sharing a struggle is not the same as complaining. Put a positive spin on the post whenever possible and never, ever complain about your group members or the number of questions you are getting. It is best to only share struggles you have overcome.

As hard as it is to share your struggles, sharing your failures is even more difficult. I know this better than anyone. When I was hired by my first airline, I was over the moon. I made it through seven and a half weeks of training and finally graduated. I started working and traveling the world as soon as they pinned those shiny new flight attendant wings to my jacket. I flew to Japan, Germany, Amsterdam and San Francisco before a miscommunication with the scheduling department caused me to end up at Baltimore Airport when the flight I was scheduled to work was leaving from Dulles Airport, an hour and a half away. I was unceremoniously terminated after only about 5 weeks on the job. To say I was devastated would be an understatement, but I had learned in those few short weeks I was meant to be a flight attendant. I started applying with other airlines right away. Well, I started applying as soon as the tears stopped flowing. It only took a few weeks before I was hired by another major airline. I went on to have a successful and rewarding career as a Continental Airlines flight attendant. I even had the opportunity to become an FAA certified in-flight instructor for PSA Airlines.

When I first started my Facebook group, I was nervous to come clean about my failure. In fact, I conveniently left the entire story out of my first book. I felt like if I showed any sort of shortcoming or weakness, it would discredit me as an authority. I was completely wrong and when I finally fessed up, the exact opposite happened. I remember the moment I was forced to choose between saving face and telling the whole truth. I am so glad I chose to be vulnerable because when I began to share my story, it started a lot of unexpected conversations. Once people heard my road had been rough and rocky, they could no longer chalk my success up to dumb luck. I had worked hard, failed, worked hard again, and succeeded. My story gives hope to those who are struggling.

Dave Ramsey, the leading authority on dumping debt and building wealth, has what could be argued as one of the most committed tribes of followers in recent history and he is generous with both the successes and the failures in his story. I'm sure now that he has told his sad story of bankruptcy and almost losing his marriage for the last 20 plus years, it doesn't smart as much as it did the first time. I imagine he too came to a place where he had to decide if he would, as a financial expert, tell the world his story of hardship and reveal all of his failures. The hope that his story brings, now that he is a millionaire, is immeasurable, but the pain he felt as he walked through the total devastation of his life was nothing to smile about. Even though the first couple of times your share your story it will hurt, it does get easier. I've found that allowing people to see your lowest moments encourages them that there is a light at the end of the tunnel. It can also be cathartic for you as the storyteller and bring purpose to your pain. Do not be afraid to share your story.

Am I a Fraud?

There is another thing I want you to be ready for as you set up your authority: feeling weird. As you establish yourself as an expert it will sometimes feel awkward or egotistical to be the one who always has an answer. If you take my advice and answer all the questions posted in your Facebook group at one time, you may be afraid that you will come across as a know-it-all, but in reality, only a handful of people will see each answer. No one will see all your answers, and even if they do, it is because they are reading every single question and every single answer. The only reason anyone would do this is to learn, so it is to your benefit to ensure all questions are answered. When questions are posted on your page, it is your responsibility to make sure they are answered. Don't feel like you are the one who has to supply all the answers, but you need to make sure the answers are there. If someone else gets to the question before you, that's great, but do not leave your members hanging. You are the expert and they will be honored to hear from you. Think about the times you have sent out a tweet or posted on Facebook and the company or the celebrity you tagged responded. I know this has happened to me before and I was over the moon excited that I had gotten a response from someone I felt was way out of my coolness league. You are the cool one in this scenario and your response will feel normal to you and super cool to your tribe. When you know the answer, share it. When you think a post is great, "Like" it. Be confident in what you know. Confidence inspires trust and trust is the backbone of any relationship.

Website and Email List

This book is about using a Facebook group to build relationships, convert customers, create fame and make money. But just like everything else in business, there is no guarantee and there is no straight path. Gathering your customers together in one place, your Facebook group, will allow you to connect with them in new and profitable ways. But don't limit yourself to using Facebook as the only way you connect.

Think about your own life and 3-D relationships. How many ways do you have to contact the people in your life? When I want to get information to my husband, I can call or text his cell phone, or I could send him a Facebook message, or I could call him at work, or I could send him an email to one of his two email accounts. The primary way we communicate is through Facebook because it shows up on the computer and on our cellphones, but if Facebook went away, or changed the rules, I could still get in touch with him.

The same is true for your business relationships. Collecting email addresses is a must. Let me say it a different way. You must collect email addresses! What if Facebook changes the rules? You have worked so hard building relationships and converting customers. All that capital is yours, not Facebook's. You need to back up your contacts and have a solid email list. I did not start collecting email addresses when I started my Facebook group. My list is tiny compared to the size of my group, but I am vigilant about collecting addresses now.

I try to reach out to my email list once a week or so. The more places you appear the better your odds are of converting them into a customer. My emails are not very long. I include links to any new blog post I've published on the website, or share an inspiring picture. From time to time, we have "breaking news" in the aviation world. When Delta started accepting flight attendant applications, I emailed the link to their career site to my entire list. The response was great. I also use the email list to send out an invitation to watch my monthly free webinar.

There are several great companies that make it easy to organize your list and send out professional emails. I use MailChimp for my list. It is free to set up an account and use most of their features. As your list grows or if you want to use some of the advanced features, such as automation, there is a small monthly fee.

Automation, sometimes called an autoresponder, is the only advanced feature I use at this time. When someone subscribes to my email list, MailChimp responds automatically with a special email that I wrote specifically for new subscribers. My autoresponder is an email that welcomes the new subscriber and includes a link to the freebie I promised. Most successful email list builders give something away to a new subscriber. These giveaways can be anything from a free eBook to a free coaching session to a free widget. My free gift is an interview worksheet which is a one-page document containing seven flight attendant interview questions. It was simple to make but is a helpful gift for a new subscriber.

The thing I love the most about MailChimp is how very user friendly it is. To collect email addresses, all you need to do is share in your Facebook group the link provided by MailChimp. I usually post the link with a short call to action. For example: "Sign up for the email list so you don't miss a thing! Plus, you'll receive a free interview worksheet when you do." I invite the members of my group to join the list every day or so. That may sound like a lot, but remember, my group grows by at least twenty people a day. So by the second day, I have fifty new members who have never been invited and that doesn't include the other members who may have missed the invite before. It is also easy to include a small sign-up form on each page of your website. That way you won't miss any opportunities to grow your list.

The second non-Facebook tool you need to pay attention to is your website. A nice website will validate you and your business just in case someone thinks you are the snake oil salesman of Facebook groups. I have a WordPress website. If you do not yet have a website, I recommend you use WordPress, too. They have lots of ways to customize your site to fit your style and the needs of your business. If you are new to WordPress, there are plenty of tutorials to guide you, or you can hire a virtual assistant, which is what I did.

Right now, I use my website to describe my products and services, publish blog posts and connect people to airlines. Taking your time and writing out a thoughtful description for all your product and services can save you time and energy later. Sometimes it's easier to just share a link with someone than it is to type the description of this thing or that every time you are asked about something. I have my pricing on my website for ease and transparency's sake. I also have a blog on the Flight Attendant Career Connection website. My goal is to post twice a week, but that doesn't always happen. When I do publish a blog post, I always share it over in the Facebook group. I also have a special page on my website. The airline listing page has a list of airlines from around the world. When a visitor clicks on the name of an airline, they are taken to that airline's career page. The Airline Listing tab is what most of my visitors come to see, which makes it a valuable tool for converting customers. Do not forget to include an opportunity to sign up for the email list on each and every page of your website. If your business model lends itself to blogging in the more traditional sense, you will love the book Everything But the Posts by Becca Ludlum.

Convert People

What do you think of when you hear the term "internet marketing?" If you are like a lot of people you think "spam." In fact, you have already read an entire section in this book about the rampant spammers that will try to infiltrate your space and convert your members into their customers. Because of the barrage of advertisements that come screaming at you from every direction, you may find yourself shying away from advertising in your group at all. Please don't think advertising, marketing, and selling are negative words. Once you have built relationships and established yourself as an authority, you must talk about what you are selling if you want to start making money.

Still uncomfortable selling? Let me ask you a few questions.

"Do you believe that you have something wonderful to offer?"

"Do you believe your products or services can make the lives of your member's better?"

If the answer to these questions is "yes" and you do not let your followers know you have all this awesomeness available to them, then you are doing your customers a huge disservice. If your customer purchases an inferior product from your competitor because you didn't make it clear you had a product that was better, you are harming your customer. That's not fair to them. Honor their trust by offering the best solution to their problem. More often than not, the solution will be found on your product list.

Let's talk about spam. No, not the canned meat product. The other spam. Here's how Dictionary.com defines spam: disruptive messages, especially commercial messages, posted on a computer network or sent as e-mail. Look at the first word in that definition: disruptive. If you are talking about and suggesting your products in a way that is not disruptive, you are not spamming. If you are being generous with your answers and then directing people to a place where they can learn even more, you are not spamming. If you are building relationships and connecting with people in a way that is real and not "all business", you are not spamming. Honestly, some people may not want to hear what you have to say, but they are not your customer and are free to move on. That's the great thing about free market. If they aren't liking what you're selling, they can move along.

Now that I have proven that talking about your business is not spamming, let's talk about some practical steps to marketing, selling, and converting customers inside your Facebook group. One of the best ways to talk about what you are selling is at the end of an answer. For example, I get asked a lot about the type of questions one might be asked to answer at a flight attendant interview. My answer usually looks something like this:

"Be ready to talk about specific times you've given great customer service, solved a problem and worked as a member of a team. Most airlines are looking for answers in the STAR format, which means they are really specific stories. You can find some sample questions on the FACC website and FACC also offers an interview workbook with over 30 questions and some instruction on the STAR format. AND THEN I PUT THE LINK."

In this example, I answered the question and even told her where she could go to find more answers. I bet she Googles the STAR format. My link to the product doesn't feel like I'm hard selling anything, but I know something she doesn't know yet. It is very difficult to find clear instruction on the STAR format which makes my workbook and the instruction it provides valuable.

The great thing about using your Facebook group to market and convert customers is once you have converts, you have an army of brand ambassadors bragging about your business. Once my answer is posted, it is usually followed by more comments from other members endorsing the workbook or even suggesting my interview coaching. Your members probably won't take the time to post links to your products and services, that's up to you, but they will be excited to talk about how awesome your products are.

Another way to market inside your Facebook is by creating a challenge. Every week or so, I ask my group what they are doing to reach their goal of becoming a flight attendant with a post that sounds like this:

"Good Morning, Dreamers!
What are you doing this week to move you closer to your goal?
Applying to three new airlines?
Revamping your resume so it's airline ready?
Practicing your STAR format?
Working out and eating right?
Creating a budget?

Reading a book?

Booking a coaching session?

I'm working on getting the blog caught up with the show notes from last week's webinar…What are you doing?"

I don't know if you caught it, but I listed every one of my products and services in those questions. I charge for resume rewrites and coaching, and I sell two books. I also mention the monthly webinar, which is free. Now that post sounds pretty inspiring and not spammy at all. You may have noticed I did not include any links in this post and might be wondering why. I think in a post this long, the links would be "noisy." I really do want people to be inspired and not distracted by product links. Another reason I didn't include any links is because I know my tribe. As they begin to comment, they will begin selling for me. One person will comment something, then another, then someone will tag me and post, "Abbie Unger, I need coaching this week!" Boom! Customer converted. I comment back, "I'd love to help you this week, send me a PM and we'll set it up." Other comments will rave about my book and I may get a question or two about resume rewrites.

Corie Clark created a challenge that caused huge growth in her group and drove up her book sales. Remember Corie's book, The Simplicity Project, is about winning the battle with chaos and clutter so you can live a life of peace and purpose. When her group was only a few weeks old, she created the *6-Week Declutter Challenge*. Every day for six weeks she posted a different decluttering challenge in her Facebook group. Right from the start, people were excited about the challenge and they shared the sign-up link on their Facebook page and invited friends. Even though the challenge is free, and the book was not required, a lot of those friends bought books. Throughout the challenge, everyone is working on a similar project and they were able to easily connect with each other and encourage each other in the Facebook group. The information for this challenge was available in the Facebook group or through email. The beauty of the Facebook group is her members could post pictures. They help each other solve problems and encourage each other when someone falls behind. Most of all, they can cheer for each other's victories. Some of her members may have felt uncomfortable posting their before and after declutter photos on their own Facebook page, but sharing the photos in a group where everyone was working toward a common goal, was liberating. Again, this is why you want to set your group to "closed" when you are setting up the privacy settings. Corie is now working on her next planner and other products to help people simplify their lives and live with purpose. Guess who can't wait to buy her next product? Her ever growing Facebook group!

From time to time, I post a straight up advertisement in my group. I'll post a picture of my book with a link to the page where it can be purchased along with the description, "If you haven't yet read Looking Skyward, I recommend you do. No matter where you are in your FA journey, this book will help you! I cover everything from what to put in your resume to what to wear to the interview. Plus it's a small investment in your future because the book is only $10." I would consider this an advertisement because there is no value besides the fact that I'm directing people to the place where they can find the answers they are looking for. I would never post this as an answer to a question.

As you learn how your group operates, you will discover what works best and what falls flat. Remember, it's all about ratios. You want to post with a ratio of about 90% content and 10% advertising. That's why I want you to always offer value in your answers. A great answer affords you the opportunity to sell later. Don't feel like all your posts have to be completely on topic. Every six weeks or so, I'll ask a question or post a comment that is way out in left field, but I know it's something my members will enjoy or get a kick out of. Doing something silly or fun like this from time to time helps your content to advertising ratio and it helps build relationship.

I've given you several ways to market and sell without coming across as spammy. I'm sure you will be able to think of even more ways to advertise to your group. Announce your new products as they become available or publicly thank one of your members for the great review they left you online. Stay present and your members will know where to find you when they are ready to buy. Be generous with your knowledge and they will be more than happy to be converted to a customer.

Convert Businesses

Now that I have built a large platform and my sphere of influence is getting bigger, I am in a position to work with other businesses. I am always on the lookout for companies that might be interested in renting my platform for a fee. In other words, I take on businesses as sponsors or advertisers and present their products and services to the members of my group, the readers of my blog, and the subscribers on my email list. I am always on the lookout for new partners. Sometimes I find them accidentally spamming the group. Sometimes I see an amazing product that I think would be perfect and sometimes I go searching for companies that I think would fit my niche and are looking for a place to advertise.

Although, I am always looking for new opportunities, I have worked hard and put a lot of blood, sweat, and tears into building my brand and earning the trust of my followers. Okay, maybe no blood, but I can assure you there were tears. The trust my followers put in me is very important to me and I protect it. Before I let anyone post an ad in my group for anything, I talk to the person who is posting and I check out the product or service that they would like to feature. I do not charge for every single advertising post that I let appear on my page, but I do check every one of them out. Once, I had a casting company contact me because they were looking to cast flight attendants in an upcoming show. I talked with the casting agent and checked out her website to make sure everything was on the up and up. In the end, I thought it was an interesting opportunity for the members of my group, so I posted about it. I did not charge the casting agency in this case because I saw the value in the fun opportunity.

Remember how we talked about the best way to handle accidental spammers? If someone, who owns a legitimate business, posts an ad in your group, you need to not only remove the post, but contact the person who posted it. I contact people if I delete their post for three reasons: it is the nice thing to do, I don't want them to re-post thinking the post had been deleted accidentally, and I want to do business with them. The message I send looks a little something like this:

"Hi! I'm Abbie, the admin over at Flight Attendant Career Connection. I saw the ad you posted in the group. This looks like a neat opportunity and I would love to know more. I'm very careful of the ads that I let go in the group and I like to check everything out before it is presented to my followers. My group trusts me and I take that seriously. Plus I have some companies who advertise for a fee and I want to be fair to them. I do work with businesses from time to time if I feel like they offer something my followers would be interested in. Please let me know more and let's talk about working together."

This post is usually met with an apology. They have no idea Flight Attendant Career Connection is a business and I make sure they know I'm not upset in any way. I usually tell them that as a small business owner myself, I respect their hustle and I offer several different sponsorship options. Some are as simple as a blog post with a review. And some are as big as a large monetary sponsorship. Some small businesses are not in a position to pay for advertising so in that case I offer them a blog post giveaway. Once a month, host a giveaway on the blog. I use this post to introduce my readers to a new company or product that I think they would benefit from. The company I feature provides the giveaway. For example, InFlight Skincare sent me several products so I could try them and review them in a blog post. They also sent a set of products to giveaway. This campaign was successful because I was able to actually review the products. One month I featured a travel club. They were not able to give away any of their product, so instead we gave away a $50 gift card. One of my first sponsors was The Flight Attendant Shop. I wrote a post in the Flight Attendant Career Connection blog, as well as, a different post in my personal blog. Now, whenever someone in my group asks me where they should buy luggage, my answer is always The Flight Attendant Shop.

As your group and your level of influence grows, so will your opportunities to partner with more and more companies. This can be an exciting way to earn passive income, but be careful. First, remember all the hard work you put in to grow your platform and earn the trust of your members. That trust matters and you would not want to do anything to jeopardize it. Research the company you are partnering with and make sure they are doing what they say they do. Don't partner with a company that is not relevant or doesn't offer something that would help your members. Secondly, honor your agreement with the companies you chose to partner with. Do not make promises you can't keep and follow through on your word. If you promise a blog post and five Facebook mentions, deliver. As you begin to work with more companies, you will come up with a system that works for you and your followers. Maybe your followers would love a giveaway, or maybe they would rather have a coupon code. Try a few things out and before you know it you'll be converting those small businesses and accidental spammers into customers.

Affiliate Sales

Another way to partner with businesses and make money is by using affiliate links. Affiliate sales may be new to you, but they are quickly gaining popularity with advertisers as well as companies. Once you learn how to use affiliate marketing effectively, an affiliate relationship can be a win-win relationship. With an affiliate relationship, unlike a traditional advertising relationship, the responsibility for selling is shared. In a more traditional relationship, the company pays for advertising and crosses their fingers as they wait for a return on investment while the advertiser works to drive sales and increase profits. Hopefully, all expectations are met and the company renews the advertising contract.

On the other hand, with this type of relationship, the company stands to gain the most. Once you accept an advertiser and negotiate a fee, the amount of money you will collect from that company during that contract period is locked in. Of course, if the sales are phenomenal, you will be able to negotiate a higher advertising fee the next go around, but ultimately there will eventually be a cap on the amount of money you can earn from that advertiser.

With an affiliate relationship the risk, as well as the reward, is shared between the two parties. As an affiliate for a company, you will recommend products to your tribe and as sales are made, the company will pay you a percentage of their earnings. You can expect to earn anywhere from 4% to 40% depending on the size of the company you are representing. The advertising company doesn't have to pay a fee upfront and hope for sales and the affiliate's payday isn't limited by a pre-negotiated fee. Making money through affiliate sales is easier than ever, and the payouts are getting bigger. Online marketers are making anywhere from a few hundred dollars a month all the way up to millions a year. Everyone from entrepreneurs like Pat Flynn from Smart Passive Income and John Lee Dumas from Entrepreneur on Fire to bloggers like Michael Hyatt are using affiliate links to supplement the sale of their own products and services and easily increase their profits.

I bet you're wondering how a company knows you have made a sale for them and when to pay you. It has to do with embedded codes and cookies and other technical stuff, but basically, you will be assigned a special code that will automatically be added to the link or web address of the product you are sharing. When someone clicks on the link you shared, they are taken to the web page containing product and ordering information. This page looks like a normal page to your customer, but the computer has tracked your referral and any purchases made will be credited to your account. Guess what else. You are not limited to earning a commission just on the product you recommended but on all the products purchased by your referred customer. You will need to read the terms of the agreement for each company you choose to represent as an affiliate, but most companies will require you reach a certain threshold, usually $25 to $100, before they send you your earnings. Once the threshold is reached, you will receive a direct deposit into your bank account.

Are you ready to start making money as an affiliate? Here's how to become an affiliate advertiser. First, pick a company you would like to work with and find their affiliate information. A lot of the time you can find the link to the affiliate page at the bottom of the home page or on the "about" page. You can also use the search bar within the website. A company usually runs their affiliate program one of two ways. They either host the program themselves or use an outside company such as Commission Junction. Commission Junction, and companies like it, manage the affiliate programs for lots of different companies. Once you sign up, you will have access to a dashboard to help you manage your affiliate programs. You will also have the ability to search through their database to find new companies to represent. Other websites, like Amazon and Groupon, keep their affiliate programs in-house.

Each company has different criteria to join their affiliate team. Some companies require a certain number of followers and others will ask a simple, "How do you plan to market our product?" All companies will have some sort of approval process. Once you are approved, you will receive the information and instructions you need to ensure your special affiliate code is embedded in the links you share with your Facebook group, email list, and other followers.

Disclosure: Because you receive compensation, affiliate links are considered ads and per FTC regulations, these posts must be identified as such. You may have noticed the disclosure I included in the description for Flight Attendant Career Connection.

Disclosure: Some of the products suggested in the group are affiliate links, which means FACC receives a commission from the sale of these items.

According to the Federal Trade Commission, the disclosure must start with the word "disclosure," be clearly stated, and be visible. You should also include a disclosure in any post containing an affiliate link. For a post, using a hashtag followed by the word "ad" or "affiliate" is fine. This is a legal issue, so please be vigilant and let your audience know you are getting a kickback. Most of the time, your followers will be happy to support your business without having to spend any extra money. I know I am always happy to use an affiliate link and give back whenever I am purchasing a product.

One of the best things about using affiliate links to make money is it doesn't change your customer's experience. When affiliate links are properly placed, they feel more like a helpful convenience than an advertisement. For example, last week during my free monthly webinar, I was asked by a viewer what color lipstick I was wearing. I didn't know off the top of my head and let the viewer know I would find out and post the answer in the Facebook group. After the webinar was complete, I grabbed the tube of lipstick and typed the brand and color number into the Amazon search bar. Up popped the lipstick. I used the affiliate toolbar provided by Amazon to easily share the link, which automatically included my affiliate tracking code, in my Facebook group. The members of my group were excited to learn what color I was wearing and appreciated the easy purchase link. This "ad" didn't feel spammy at all. And remember, I will earn a percentage not only from every tube of lipstick I sell but all the other products purchased once my customer clicks on my link. Because of the Christmas shopping season, November and December are the best months for Amazon affiliate sales.

Another strategy for sharing an affiliate link without it coming across as spam is to couple a product with a tip, inside information, or feedback regarding the product. I have found success sharing travel or packing tips along with an affiliate link to the product mentioned in the tip. One thing flight attendants are always looking for is food packing tips. Traveling for work four days in a row, twenty days a month can make affordable, healthy eating a challenge. Because I know this is a problem, whenever I see leak-proof food storage containers for sale on Groupon, I share the link with a food tip or two. Because of the report provided by Groupon, I can tell that this post gets clicked on a lot and I usually sell a few sets of storage containers. Now, a 4% commission on a few $24.99 food storage sets isn't much, but sometimes I sell more than just the food storage set. A few months ago, I had a customer click on my Groupon link, purchase a food storage set, and a $2000 teeth whitening service. I made almost $200 on that sale! I know $200 isn't going to pay the rent, but an extra $200 isn't bad for a Facebook post that took five minutes.

Here are some more tips for making money with affiliate links.

1) Become an affiliate for as many companies as you can. Because of the win-win aspect of affiliate sales, more and more companies are offering affiliate programs. Companies like Shutterfly, Groupon, and Choice Hotels all offer affiliate programs. Your influence may not be big enough to take on a large company like Shutterfly as an advertiser, but you can still create revenue when you promote a product that your group members will find valuable.

2) Use an affiliate link whenever you can. Anytime you are talking about a product, whether in your Facebook group, a blog post, or on your personal social media feed, include an affiliate link. Even if the product is inexpensive, it is still worth it to grab a link from Amazon before sharing. I have even made money from suggesting free eBooks offered by Amazon. Once a customer clicks on my affiliate link, I earn a commission on anything they buy. Don't forget to always use an affiliate link every time you post about a product.

3) Think outside the box. Some companies do not offer a cash payment to their affiliates, but instead offer a credit for referring new customers. Uber, HotelTonight, and Stitch Fix are just a few examples. HotelTonight is one of my favorite phone apps. Because my husband works for an airline, we fly for free, but we fly standby. Even though we try to make good choices concerning the flights we choose (like not flying during spring break or the week before Christmas) from time to time, we get stuck in a connecting city overnight and we never really know if we will reach our destination on our first try. Because of our constantly up in the air travel plans, HotelTonight is perfect. The app offers last-minute hotel rooms at a huge discount and with their new feature, you can book a discounted hotel up to a week in advance. I could go on and on about why I love HotelTonight, but back to affiliates. When I refer a new customer to HotelTonight and they use my code, (Aunger4) I receive a $25 credit to use towards my next hotel stay, plus the person I refer receives a

$25 credit towards their first booking. Over the last year or so, I have earned a few hundred dollars to use towards hotel rooms. The $25 isn't cash, but it felt like cash when we were sitting next to the hotel pool in Puerto Rico.

The bottom line is the best way to make money with Facebook groups is through multiple revenue streams. Convert your members into paying customers who buy your books, products, and services. Back up the connections you make by using your email list and your website. Then, convert other businesses into sponsors and advertisers. Keep these relationships strong and healthy and you will have money flowing in from all directions in no time. Before you know it, you will have created enough fame to cause people to notice you and your success. Once this happens, you won't even have to go looking for opportunities because the opportunity will come looking for you.

CREATE FAME

It's Not Fame's Fault

When I first began talking about the title of this book, some people didn't like that I was planning on using the word fame in the title. They had a strong reaction to the idea that I would encourage business owners and authors to chase or create fame. A little negativity is to be expected, but I was surprised at the amount of pushback I got over the word fame. I am part of a special Facebook group full of small business owners, authors, creatives, and dreamers. We support each other and they are invaluable for bouncing ideas around. When they read the word "fame," it didn't sit well. I was encouraged to use a different word like influence or expertise, but none of these other words defined what I was creating quite like the word fame. When did fame become a four letter word? Okay, so it has always technically been a four-letter word, but you know what I mean. When did we start thinking of fame as a negative byproduct of success?

Fame is a funny thing. For some, it is the goal. For others, it is simply a byproduct of achieving success in one's chosen profession. For others, fame is a bad thing. For them, the thought of becoming exposed is uncomfortable. What do you think of fame? Have you always dreamed of becoming famous or has it never crossed your mind? The thought of being known by strangers can be either terrifying or exhilarating, but if you want to build something that matters, you need to prepare yourself for the fact that you will develop some level of fame. It may be kept within your industry or your acclaim could reach the national stage. How far your fame takes you is largely up to you, but you cannot stay anonymous and become a thought leader and a game changer. People need to see you, trust you, and feel as if they know you if you are going to ask them to support you, buy from you, and advocate for you.

Being well known around the Facebook group will help you build those relationships and convert customers more easily. As your group of followers begins to grow and as your words begin to affect and influence people in a way that enables the creation of positive change, you will experience some level of fame. Every single one of you will experience fame in one form or another. I want you to be ready for it. Does the thought of fame disgust or excite you? Really think about it. I want you to become prepared to receive your adoring fans and passionate brand ambassadors. It is important you don't let them down or try to hide from them.

Fame is not limited to singers and athletes, just look at the Kardashians. They have created notoriety and more importantly, influence by staying in the spotlight. The fame the Kardashian brand created has opened doors that would have been out of reach if not for their ability to harness fame and turn it into influence. As much as they sometimes get a bad rap, the Kardashian family is full of savvy business women who have leveraged fame into a clothing line, licensing deals, and endorsements resulting in millions of dollars.

Because of the Kardashians, Snookie and other outrageous characters who have become famous for the sake of becoming famous, we sometimes think of fame as a negative side effect of success. We shy away from the spotlight because we don't want to be labeled a media hound or accused of seeking out the limelight. We stand to the side and humbly suggest that our work should stand alone. We shrug off the recognition. If this sounds like you, Stop it! Fame is not bad, negative, or something that should be avoided. Someone is going to end up famous. Why not you?

☐

Fame! I'm Going to Live Forever

Fame is a powerful tool. Dictionary.com defines fame as *"widespread reputation, especially of a favorable character; renown."* What is so bad about that? Being renowned, especially because of your favorable character should be something you are chasing. Not fame for fame's sake, but fame for reputation's sake. Fame is amoral. Sure, some people have abused fame, but fame is not inherently good or evil.

Think of a car. A car is amoral. On its own it is not good or bad. A car could be used to transport the sick to a hospital. Cars allow us to connect with friends and family that live far away. Cars get us to work, church, and school. But a car is not good. A car can be loaded with explosives and used to kill. But a car is not bad. The car is not moral, the car is amoral. Humans are the ones who decide if a car is going to be used to help or to destroy. What you do with fame is up to you, but fame is not going to do anything to you that it doesn't have permission to do. Fame is not something to be feared or avoided, but appreciated and embraced. Leverage your fame to open doors you never imagined.

Have I convinced you to do a little fame chasing? Yes? No? Maybe? Whether you have come to terms with the thought of fame or not, fame is coming for you. You may not end up chased by the paparazzi or with your face splashed across the cover of People magazine. That type of fame is largely up to you to encourage or avoid. Your fame may be smaller. A lot smaller. Do not define fame by how recognizable your name is to the general public. Your fame will be measured by how many people in your target audience know you. Are you a thought leader in your industry? Are you on the cutting edge of change? Are you a guide, paving the way? Are your words connecting with readers? Are you generous with your time and resources? These are the things that create fame.

In the aspiring flight attendant industry, I am famous. My name is recognized, my words are quoted, and my products are endorsed by happy customers. My name is dropped in forums and at flight attendant interviews. I am sought out to attend flight attendant training graduations by people I have never met. People ask to take pictures with me. From time to time, I am even recognized by a stranger in the airport. My advice stands as truth and my opinion carries weight. Even though I am famous within the world of aviation, I am not a celebrity recognized by the general public. In fact, you may not have even heard of me before my book popped up as an Amazon suggestion, but in my area of specialty, I am famous.

My goal is to become known outside of the world of aspiring flight attendants so I am leveraging the press and PR that comes my way into more and more opportunities. When Facebook featured my group and my business in Facebook Stories, it created a splash that swelled into a tidal wave of opportunity. Mashable.com interviews, Huffington Post articles, podcast interviews. I have even been a guest on an Australian morning show. As I am writing this, I am in final talks with a reality show. That may or may not happen right now, but the opportunity came directly from my Facebook group. For me, People magazine is the goal. You might limit the level of fame you create to being a thought leader in your industry.

When my acclaim began to grow, I was unsure about how I should act. I feel like I'm just a regular girl who is passionate about aviation and passionate about helping people make their dreams come true, but people don't seek out the help of regular girls and follow their advice. And they don't buy books written by regular girls. People seek out experts. Publishing a book used to define you as an expert, but that is quickly changing. Now it is fame that defines you as an expert and that is why it is so important to nurture and embrace fame as it comes your way.

What does it mean to embrace fame? First, don't dismiss the accolades. Thank people for endorsing you, for posting about and reviewing you. Thank your tribe for rallying around you and believing in your message. We've all seen the pop star thank her fans from the Grammy stage. Follow suit and thank your fans from your stage. When one of my members receives a job offer or graduates from flight attendant training, they will post a thank you in the Facebook group. I always thank them and tell them how proud of them I am, but I don't downplay my part in their success. These shout outs introduce me and my name to new members who may not have been converted into customers yet. The little bit of fame helps me make more money.

The second way you can embrace fame is by validating it. You validate fame by sharing your successes. When you have a big win, tell your tribe and let them spread the good news. When your book comes out, talk about it. When one of your clients does something amazing, brag a little. When you are quoted in an article, post the link and share it. Your tribe will already think you have something amazing to offer, and it is exciting for them to see their support validated by your successes.

Thirdly, enjoy the fame. Even if you are uncomfortable being the center of attention or accepting compliments, do your best to enjoy your moment in the sun. People are looking at you because you have done something that has solved a problem or inspired them. Enjoy the compliments and the five-star reviews. Enjoy the praise and recognition.

Let your reputation become widespread within your industry. Let your favorable character become known. Let your products, words, and brand become renowned. Embrace fame and live famously.

But It Feels Funny

As you begin to gain some name recognition, a strange thing will begin to happen. You will feel funny about the new found admiration. Even though you have been showing up in your group, writing blog posts, and doing everything in your power to get your name and the name of your company noticed, when all your hard work pays off, it will feel a little odd. When my name started popping up around the internet, in Facebook groups I was not a part of, and on job search forums, it felt strange. To be completely honest, the little voice of fear was whispering in my ear and telling me I was a fraud. I just knew I was going to be found out as an imposter at any time. I had positioned myself as the expert, I had even written a book to prove I was an expert, but as soon as I was received as an expert, the doubts started to creep in. I found myself wanting to downplay what I had achieved and shrug off the compliments from my members and clients. If I had not realized I was subconsciously reacting negatively to the success, I could have sabotaged everything I had built with just a few destructive behaviors. Now I am used to being quoted and turned to as the expert. That does not mean I do not appreciate the respect. When I sit back and look at what I have accomplished, I am truly in awe and I will be eternally grateful to those first dozen or so Facebook group members who really believed in me and what I was trying to build. Even as I sit here typing I can see their faces in my head and I am so indebted to those brave dreamers. Just because I am becoming comfortable in my little bit of fame, I do not take it for granted.

I am telling you about the emotional side of fame because I want you to be ready for it. I also want to give you some suggestions on how to deal with this new found recognition. First, stay the course. Don't stop doing what you're doing. Don't stop commenting and posting. Don't stop "liking" everything. When I post in the Facebook group and my post is commented on, I "like" the comment. In fact, I "like" every single comment that is made on my post. I try to think about how I would feel if someone I thought was famous "liked" my comment, or worse, "liked" other comments, but skipped mine. I probably won't always be able to "like" everything, but for now I can. Interacting in the group the same way I always have helps me get over the weirdness and reminds me I am doing good work.

Another way to deal with feeling like a fraud is to acknowledge how you are feeling. At first, you may start feeling uncomfortable or afraid for no clear reason. Everything will be going great, relationships are being built and customers are being converted, but you just can't shake this feeling of impending doom. This in normal. Did you hear that? Let me say it again. This is normal! Take a few deep breaths and acknowledge that being recognized is weird, but it is okay. As long as you are always upfront and honest, you have nothing to be afraid of. As long as you are not presenting yourself as something that you are not, you are not a fraud and, therefore, will not be uncovered as a fraud. Now take another deep breath and smile. You are doing things right and it is working. Congratulations.

Once the media starts to take notice and as you become known in your niche, you will probably be approached with opportunities outside of your area of expertise or outside of your area of concentration. Be careful as you decide what new projects you are going to take on and what you are going to turn down. When the Facebook Stories article came out, I was approached by another self-published author. She asked me if I would be willing to consult with her concerning getting her book sales up. I really wanted to help her. I had read her book even before she contacted me and I loved it already. I was excited to talk with her. Her focus was on selling her self-published books. I have sold more copies than the average self-published author, but I haven't sold a million. The more I thought about it, the more I realized, I didn't want to take my coaching skills in that direction and I may not be the best person to help her reach her particular goals. I wrote her an email explaining my feelings and she was thankful I had been so thoughtful in considering the opportunity. Instead of taking her on as a client, I am taking her on as a friend. We plan to get together soon to bounce ideas off each other. Remember to stay true to your feelings and don't let all the opportunities that fame brings slow you down or distract you from your goals. Every time you are contacted, build a relationship, but you do not have to convert every customer. Be wise as you say, "Yes." Saying, "No" up front is much easier than saying "I'm sorry" later.

As you are sifting through the opportunities that head your way and judging them against your brand and your goals, don't become too rigid in your goal chasing that you don't take advantage of the good surprises that come your way. A few weeks ago, I received an email from a casting agent. She was looking to cast two flight attendants for a new survival show on National Geographic and had stumbled upon my Facebook group in one of her searches. Before she reached out to me, I had never considered doing anything quite like that before, but it looked like an interesting opportunity. Even though my goal is not to become a survivalist expert, this show is offering me a place on a national stage and highlighting my flight attendant experience. At this point, all the B-roll has been filmed and the interviews completed. I don't know if my partner and I made the cut, but either way, this has been a fun thing to pursue. Without my Facebook group, this opportunity would never have come knocking. Without my openness to pursuing new and surprising possibilities this opportunity might have passed me by.

Fan the Flames

Getting noticed by the media is exciting and there is nothing like a little free PR, but in the end, even free PR is not really free. It takes the investment of time. Even more than that it requires that you invest effort. When social media or traditional media lights a tiny spark of acclaim, it is up to you to fan the flame. If you are not looking for fame or recognition outside of your niche, or if you are happy with the level of notoriety you have achieved, then you do not need to do anything to encourage the media. Be gracious and don't hide from the success, but you don't need to stand there fanning a fire that you don't want burning in the first place. Some of you reading this are so happy that I just let you off the hook. But some of you, those of you who are like me, you love the spotlight and get all wiggly on the inside at the thought of doing interviews and seeing your name in lights. If a little media buzz surrounding your business is one of your goals, you will need to strike while the iron is hot. One mention or a little bit of interest in one area can quickly burn out or become a blazing fire of exposure depending on how aggressively you feed the flames.

Remember how I was talking about never burning any bridges? This holds true for every kind of relationship. If you are careful and strategic, you will be able to turn one mention into an interview. Then that interview into another and another. As you begin to interact with members of the media, be especially gracious and easy to get a hold of. Respond to emails quickly. If you receive a request for an interview, find time to do it. Be extremely easy to work with and build those relationships. Make their job easier and they will be more willing to help you promote your next product or event. When I was first contacted by Facebook, I was over the moon excited. I cleared my calendar for the phone interview they requested and we talked the very next day. I felt the interview went great, but then nothing happened. I followed up from time to time and was assured Facebook did still want to feature my story, and they would be in touch soon. Finally, about three months after we first spoke, Facebook ran my story on the Facebook Stories page. I started sharing the article and I asked my Facebook group to share the story, too. Over the next few days, I was contacted by podcasts, and other members of the media for interviews. Then I received another message from my contact at Facebook. Facebook was excited about the buzz my Facebook Stories article had gotten and they would like to send a film crew to my house to film a live interview with me. If I was interested. Of course, I was interested! A few days after that message, she messaged me again. She had been contacted by Mashable.com and they were requesting my contact information to set up an interview, too. Again, I cleared a spot on my calendar for the Mashable.com interview. I am developing relationships with members of the media that will be useful to me as my business grows and changes. Plus, I am offering them great content by being readily available and generous with my story. The Huffington Post article caught the eye of a morning show in Australia. I was out shopping with my mom on my birthday when I got the media request from a producer at Mornings9. I was out and about and couldn't really talk, but I still took a few seconds and replied to her email with a big "YES, I'm out and about right now, but I would love to talk to you soon." Even though I'm not going to be available all the time, I can at least respond and show my enthusiasm.

When the media begins to call, it is okay to be a novice and ask questions, but always be professional in your correspondence and your attitude. I honestly had no idea how anything worked in the news and TV industry, and what I thought I knew was wrong. I followed directions and let the professionals handle the details. My philosophy for doing scary things is say "Yes" first and figure it out second. You would never want your nerves or apprehension to come across as disinterest or unavailability. Building relationships with everyone you come in contact with is the foundation of creating fame and making money with Facebook groups.

Another way to gain exposure and fan the flames of fame is by writing for large online publications. You may not know this, but large online publications, such as Entrepreneur.com and The Huffington Post, are always looking for contributors. These sites produce and publish so much content that they have begun to rely on what they refer to as "bloggers" to help meet the demand. Most of the time, these blogger or contributor positions are unpaid, but they offer tons of exposure. Adding "contributor to the Huffington Post" to your bio raises your expert status and having your bio, with links to your website and Facebook group, under your article exposes you to a whole new audience.

Getting an article published on one of these large websites isn't as hard as you might think. First, you need an article that is appropriate for the website you are planning on pitching. This may sound like it should go without saying, but do not write your article until you have spent some time on the website. Find out which articles have been well received by their audience. Some online publications offer excellent insight in the form of writer's guidelines but do not rely solely on the guidelines to direct your writing. Find a few similarities between the top or trending article and use them to direct your writing.

I think the hardest thing about getting published is convincing yourself to pull the trigger and submit your article. Some websites have clear, easy to find instructions on how they would like to receive submissions, but if this is not the case for the publication you are interested in writing for, submit your pitch in an email to an editor. You can usually find editor contact information by doing a Google search or using the search bar on the website. When you email your submission, start with a brief introduction that includes the article's word count and links to some of your published works. If you haven't been published yet, a few links to your most popular blog posts would work, too. If you don't have a blog or published articles, don't let that stop you from pitching.

Next, paste the entire article in the body of the email. Do not attach any files to the email. End your article with a headshot and a 2-3 sentence bio that is suitable for printing.

It may take a few tries to get one of your articles accepted for publication, but keep trying. Soon, you will be able to add "published author" to all your other awesome qualifications.

☐

Haters Gonna Hate

Have you ever noticed that sometimes people aren't very nice? I know there are plenty of people who wish only good things for others, but they don't ever seem to shout quite as loudly as those who are voicing a negative opinion. If you want to have a business and a brand that is making an impact you will need to develop a thick skin. You will need to be brave.

"Courage isn't an absence of fear. It's doing what you are afraid to do. It's having the power to let go of the familiar and forge ahead into new territory." *~John Maxwell*

I love this quote. To accomplish your goals, you will need to do things that make you uncomfortable and when I say "uncomfortable" I mean "scared." You will be going toe to toe with failure, embarrassment, and fear. You must be ready to battle. Changing the world, or even changing your family for the better is not for the faint of heart. You will be fighting to take new ground, fighting against that fear voice that whispers in your ear, and fighting against the negativity that is shot at you and your business by those who either don't understand you or are just mean, horrible people. I'm not warning you about the battle that is coming to scare you off or discourage you. I am warning you only because I want you to be ready to fight. Remember, the best defense is a good offense. I don't want the first negative comment to throw you off your game. I don't want the first rejection to make you reconsider everything you have been passionately building. Instead, I want you to get ready right now. Be strong. Be afraid. Be courageous.

There are risks involved with attempting greatness. People will attack you and the brand you are trying to build. It could be because they are jealous, because they don't understand, or because they are just miserable in their own life. But whatever the reason they chose to spew venom your way, it will feel very personal and it will hurt. The negative comment or unfounded criticism can come from almost any direction. You may receive an email or a Facebook message. Maybe someone will publish a negative review about you, your book, or the service they received from your business. Or maybe they just go straight to social media and put you on blast. No matter which direction the criticism comes from, it will hurt.

The only way to protect yourself is to take a deep breath and remind yourself of all the good you are doing. You will have to do this on purpose, and you will not feel like it. But we've already established that you really do have something great to offer, that you believe you are able to make a difference in the lives of the people who trust you. The possibility of helping someone will have to matter more to you than the harsh, fiery words that are shot at you.

Now that my group is heading towards 10,000 members, I am dealing with negativity and criticism more often. The ratio of positive people to negative people isn't changing. As the number of people in my group grows, the number of great, positive people goes up, but so does the number of negative people. Recently I had a member of my group whose comments came across a little salty. The comments would usually hurt the feeling of the question asker or offend another member who would come to the rescue and a fight would break out right there under the question, "Should I wear Pink or White to my interview?" Other members were messaging me and asking me to remove the offending member from the group. It is my policy to reach out before kicking someone out. I sent her a message asking her to be kinder, which she said she would do. She was kind for a few days and then the snark started again. I spoke to her again. She was a current flight attendant and I felt like she really had a lot to offer, but her delivery was horrible. Again, she assured me she would be kind and again, she only behaved herself for a few days. I finally had to send her a message that I had decided to remove her from the group. I'll be honest, I felt really bad about it, but her reaction quickly dissolved any remorse I had about the choice I had made. She replied by saying "At least I never got fired from an airline." She had taken the painful story I share as a way of offering hope to others and turned it into a barb. It's like she tried to think of the meanest thing she could say to try to hurt me. It was so mean it didn't even hurt my feelings. Yes, I got fired, but I went on to fly for two more carriers and I had an amazing career. I ignored the message and put her out of my mind so I could focus more on the people who wanted my help. The next day, she started posting her mean little barbs all over social media. Although I had removed her from my group, she was still free to follow me on my personal fan page, Abbie Unger: Speak. Travel. Coach. and my business fan page, Flight Attendant Career

Connection. She commented on one of my exciting media request posts by saying, "Make sure you tell them about how you got fired." Wowzers! But you know what, I have always been honest and generous with my story, so even though she thought she was going to embarrass me, everyone already knew I had been fired, so it was not breaking news.

Prepare yourself because they will come for you. The jealous, the hurt, the misunderstanding. They will come for you and attack. Some will attack accidently, and some will wage a full-on war against you and your business. But you are strong. You are fighting for the good and you have something worth protecting. Here are a few tips to help you remain brave and battle against the trolls. First, remember that your group is YOUR GROUP. You offer it as a service to your members, but they do not own it. If someone is out of line and they don't want to play by your rules, remove them from the group. I'm a softy and message everyone to give them a chance to turn it around, but my assistant is swifter with her judgment. Either way is fine, as long as at the end of the day you have the guts to set them free if they don't contribute to your group in a way that is beneficial to all. Secondly, remember it isn't really personal. It feels personal and they probably mean their insults to be personal, but really it's not personal. It can't be personal because it is happening in a virtual world. If your best friend or your husband says to you "At least I never got fired," that, my friend, is personal. A jab from a stranger on the other end of the internet is not personal. My third piece of advice to help you survive in the heat of the battle is do not read or consume feedback that is not valuable. I do not read any of the comments at the bottom of the news stories that have been written about me. I read a couple and they were so silly and critical, I knew right away they would offer no value. One commenter said she would never pay me to rewrite her resume based on my poor grammar in a Facebook post. Come on Lady, like a Facebook post is the same thing as a formal document. Some authors have their virtual assistant read any reviews they receive and forward anything of value to the author. This avoids any unnecessary pain. Another thing to consider is people who have such a strong dislike for you, your company, or your product are not your target audience. And if they are not your target audience, then you don't need them or their prickly opinion.

Creating fame comes with its own set of risks and possibilities.

From time to time, you may feel like you are living someone else's life or you may not even be able to truly grasp the magnitude of the opportunities you are presented with. Just keep knocking on doors and walking through the ones that are open. Remember the good things. Keep the compliments closer than the critics. Anything that is worth doing will be met with difficulty. No princess has ever been rescued without a dragon first being slayed.

Do It Your Way

Even though this book focuses on one primary way to use Facebook groups, the possibilities are endless. I use one large Facebook group as a way to gather my tribe into one place. My members are primarily looking for information to help them land their dream job when they visit Flight Attendant Career Connection. Your Facebook group may be different. Your members may be looking for community or discussion. If you are a fiction writer, your group may be used as a fan site where you ask for feedback on book covers and story themes. I work with aspiring flight attendants which means my members are outgoing and social by nature. They are not intimidated by the size of the group. You may find that what you are trying to accomplish is better facilitated by several smaller groups instead of one big group.

My friend Rebekah Bain, the owner of Rock Fitness, has found success using small Facebook groups. She is a Beachbody coach and is passionate about helping people live healthy lives. She also has a team of coaches under her that she faithfully trains and mentors as they build successful small businesses. Rebekah is a Facebook group master. Her system is different. She doesn't use one big group, but several little groups. Every month, she starts a new challenge group of about twenty-five people that will run for sixty days. This group has a mix of new clients, old clients, and even a few coaches. For sixty days, the members post about their exercise, food choices, and struggles. The small group allows the participants to lean on and encourage each other and gives Rebekah an easy way to get information out to her group. She can also easily check on a client that may have been quiet for a few days and she uses the other members, especially the coaches, to help her encourage anyone who is struggling. Some of the groups become so active and the members so bonded, that she will let the group continue after sixty days. Sometimes the groups are not very active, especially towards the end of the challenge. Rebekah dissolves these groups and moves her interested clients to a new group. Her model is to keep her groups small and intimate. She will probably never have a group of thousands of members, but that's not her goal. Collecting smaller tribes that she can easily monitor is how she makes money with Facebook groups.

Sometimes success is found through a hybrid approach. The large group of peers I was telling you about in the Fame section of this book is a hybrid. The large group is a central meeting place with over 2,000 members. We post and comment in the large group, but we are also active in subgroups. There is a subgroup for the men and one for the women. There is a subgroup for writers. One for designers. One for singles and one for marrieds. These subgroups allow for even more specific advice and discussion to exist while we stay connected in the big group.

As you can tell, there are so many different ways you can use a Facebook group to grow your business. One big group, several small groups, or a hybrid. You could also create a Facebook group to test a product. Bestselling author John Oakes (The Right Kind of Stupid) had an idea for a one-month program that would walk a new writer through 30 days of preparation, thus setting the writer up for success when it came time to write a novel. John started a Facebook group and offered his members a month's worth of prompts. He asked his members to share what they were working on and encouraged them to reach out to each other when the going got tough. Now that his month of prompts is over, John has a product for new novelists that has been tried and tested and is ready for sale. He also has a dedicated fan base that is grateful for his guidance and ready to tell others just how helpful his product is for the aspiring novel writer.

In the ever-changing world of marketing and social media, it can sometimes feel overwhelming to even attempt to get your message noticed. Knowing where to begin and where to invest your time can be confusing but it boils down to collecting a group of people who need what you are selling. Build relationships that inspire trust. Serve your group with generosity and they will quickly become lifelong customers. Proudly display your expertise while you remain approachable and relevant.

If you have made it this far into Make Money with Facebook Groups without creating your own group, what are you waiting for? Do it right now. Download the Facebook messenger app and the Facebook groups app onto your phone. Start posting and you are on your way. Once you get the ball rolling, I would love to hear about your success. Send me an email at **abbie.unger@gmail.com** or connect with me at **www.abbieunger.org**.

I'll tell you a little secret about those who look really successful. Even though they may look smooth from the outside looking in, they are mostly winging it, too. Just jump in and start swimming. Before you know it you will be building relationships, converting customers, creating fame, and making money with Facebook groups.

ABOUT THE AUTHOR

Abbie is a speaker and author who is passionate about helping people see their dreams come true. She is a former flight attendant with her head still in the clouds and her feet reluctantly on the ground.

Abbie's company, Flight Attendant Career Connection, offers encouragement, coaching, community, and resources to aspiring flight attendants. Her Facebook group by the same name has over 17,000 members. In June 2014, Facebook itself took notice of what she was building and featured her story.

Abbie is a go-to expert for the Huffington Post and Yahoo Travel. She has been interviewed by Mashable.com, Mornings Australia, the Charleston City Paper and other media outlets.

You can learn more about her adventures with her husband, Jason, and their three children, Ty, Emily Grace, and Jet, on her blog, www.abbieunger.org.

Abbie would love to come speak, teach, and encourage your group. Send her an email at abbie.unger@gmail.com to learn more.

Are you dreaming of becoming a flight attendant? Abbie's eBook can show you how you can make that dream a reality. Available at www.flightattendantcareerconnection.com.